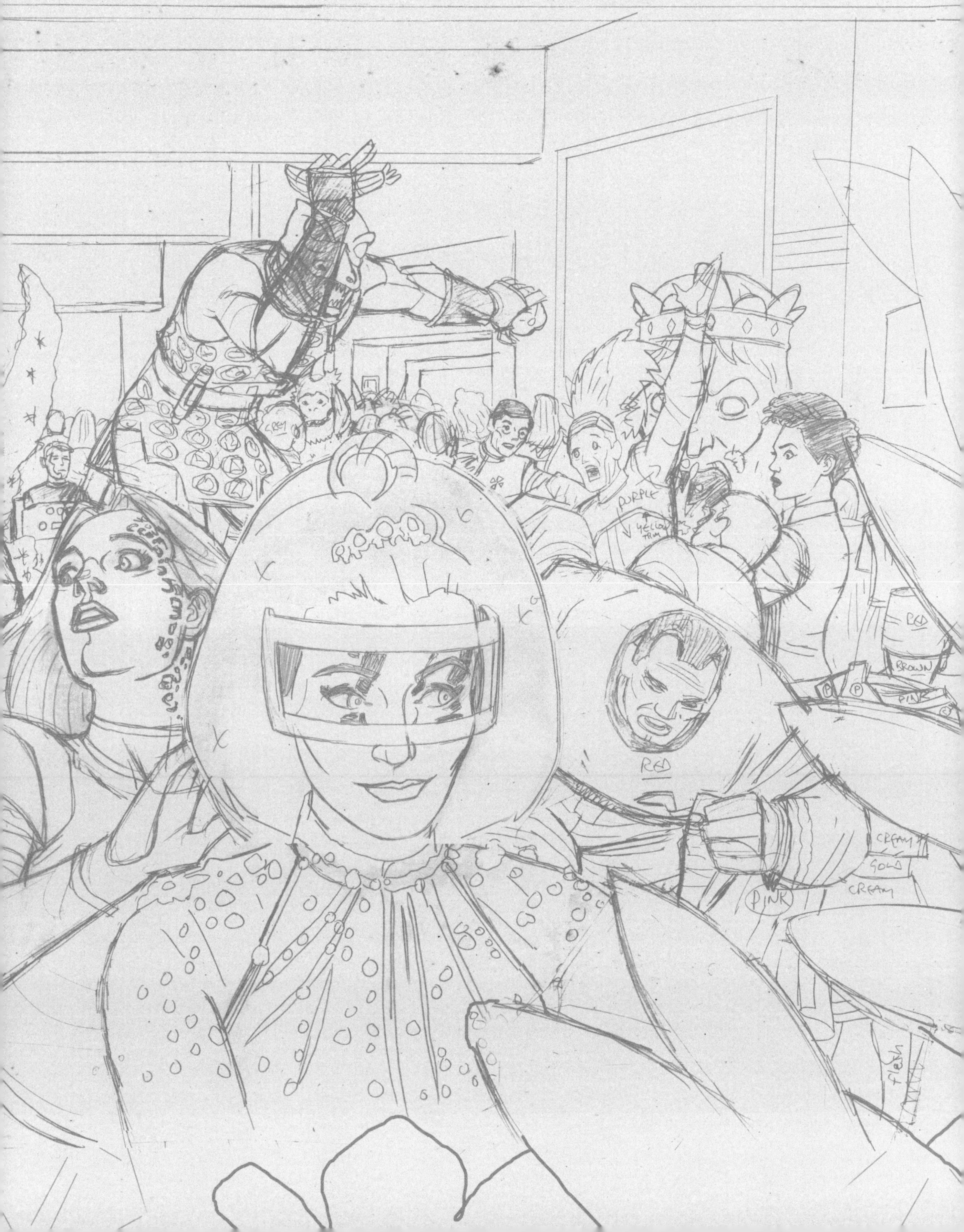
PURPLE
YELLOW TRIM
RED
BROWN
PINK
RED
CREAM
GOLD
CREAM
PINK
Flesh

Written by Glenn Dakin

Art by John Ross

Colors by Alan Craddock

Consultant Ben Robinson

eaglemoss HERO COLLECTOR

Eaglemoss Ltd. 2020

1st Floor, Kensington Village, Avonmore Road, W14 8TS, London, UK.

***W**hat is a* **Nerd Search?** It's a puzzle book, but not as you know it. We're giving you a chance to enjoy your favorite show all over again – by ruining it for you! We all love discussing our top movies and TV shows. Be honest, we even love to find fault with them. Well, here we provide the faults!

This is not your ordinary search-and-find book, but a diabolical test of your nerdular knowledge of your favorite topic. Instead of simply finding lost objects, you have to spot errors no one but an obsessive superfan could spot.

And before we go any further we have to admit this whole book is one big continuity error. The scenes in it NEVER HAPPENED. Well, not like this, anyway. We have taken classic moments and added a dire plot, and lots of other illogical elements to bamboozle you... and given you the chance to prove you're the biggest fan ever!

HOW TO USE THIS BOOK

TYPES OF PUZZLE

There are four types of puzzle in this book. The puzzles are contained in eight spreads based on classic episodes from *STAR TREK:* THE ORIGINAL SERIES.

1. TRIBBLE HUNT

Spot the **exploding tribble** before it does too much damage. It is a fiery, little, furry fiend with evil eyes, created by the Klingons.

2. NERD ALERT

Each spread has **five continuity errors**. It could be a character wearing the wrong uniform. It could be someone appearing in the scene who should not be there. It might be something un-*TREK*-like, such as a Klingon hugging a kitten. Some errors will even range out into the wider *TREK* universe!

3. THE ARTIFACT INCIDENT

The original series contained 79 different stories, including the pilot, 'The Cage,' and considering 'The Menagerie,' Parts I and II, as a single story. **One element from each of these stories** can be discovered distributed throughout the eight double page spreads. These can be anything from characters to even a poster on the wall.

4. SUPER QUIBBLES

Across the book there are **five random Super Quibbles**. They could involve behind-the-scenes knowledge, an item physically appearing in the scene that was only mentioned in dialogue, an incorrect facial expression or a quirky prop detail.

THE SCORING SYSTEM

Use your scorecard to keep track of your progress.

Answers on page 24

TRIBBLE HUNT: **7 points** each.

NERD ALERT: **4 points** each.

ARTIFACT INCIDENT: 1 point for spotting the out-of-context element and **1 point** for naming the episode it comes from. The first seven spreads have ten artifacts each, for a combined total of **47 points**. 'Amok Time' has nine artifacts, so there are **45 points** to collect. At this point, the maximum score is **374**.

BUT WAIT! With the five random **SUPER QUIBBLES**, worth **265.4 points** each, this brings the top possible score to the magic number of **1701**!

TO NERDILY GO

There is only one thing better than enjoying your favorite TV show, and that is criticizing it. It's a curious fact that many sports fans spend more time picking apart their own team than slandering the opposition and the same goes for that one TV show you love. Lambasting your adopted series reinforces your sense of caring.
We dismiss stuff we don't care about.
We criticize stuff we want to be better.

STAR TREK is an extraordinary case in point. The title sequence famously declared the starship *Enterprise* would "boldly go where no man has gone before." In terms of a TV show having a relationship with its fans, *STAR TREK* really did go where no one had gone. When *TREK* seemed doomed to cancellation after the end of Season Two in 1968, a concerted fan letter-writing campaign kept it alive for a third series. This forged a link between fans and show that has never died.

FIRST TREK CON

There had been fan conventions in the USA before, celebrating science fiction, for example, but *STAR TREK* came to own the concept in a new way. The first *TREK* con was in Newark, New Jersey in 1969, but the first one with guests took place in New York in 1972. Anticipating several hundred fans at most, they were swamped with more than 3,000, packing a ballroom to hear series' creator Gene Roddenberry answer questions about a show that had already been canceled. The conventions and the show have grown together ever since.

STAR TREK seems to bring out the nerd in people, its serious approach to a far-fetched subject challenging even devotees to spot the cracks in the perfection. In its early days, the show entertained, but also raised questions in audiences more used to the limitations of horses and Colt 45s than warp drive and phasers.

PRIME DIRECTIVE

"Since they can beam them into trouble, why don't they just beam them out again?" casual viewers would say, missing such nuances as atmospheric disturbance. Also, if Spock can mind-meld with people, why doesn't he do it every time the crew requires information? An ongoing smirk was inspired by the Federation's prime directive of non-interference in alien cultures. Quite frankly, interfere was all Kirk and his merry crew ever did.

Gene Roddenberry's commitment to creating a fully-realized and consistent imaginary world lent the show a fascination that invited affectionate nit-picking. In the second pilot episode, 'Where No Man Has Gone Before,' Captain James Tiberius Kirk is shown his future tombstone: James R. Kirk.

In 'Charlie X' (S1.2), Kirk enters a lift in a gold captain's top and emerges in a green V-neck shirt. White furry slippers are seen on Yeoman Rand's feet in the same show, then instantly vanish.

VULCAN MOON

The classic 'The City On The Edge Of Forever' (S1.28) episode time-traveled to the 1930s to show a sign indicating the presence of a fall-out shelter, 30 years before they existed. In the same episode a derelict is seen with an amputated finger, which he regrows for a close-up quickly afterwards. In its very first broadcast episode 'The Man Trap' (S1.1), Spock tells Uhura that Vulcan has no moon. Yet in the first movie, one was clearly seen in Vulcan's sky (and later erased on the DVD release).

It isn't unusual that these mistakes occurred in a TV show. It is unusual that people cared.

Sometimes, the fan blowback was not for literal mistakes, but perceived errors of approach. Gene Roddenberry reported in a memo on Season Three that the biggest single complaint from all age groups was that Spock and McCoy had stopped arguing. Their banter had become a valued 'norm' in an outlandish future context. When the TV show was canceled their arguments were restored in the movies, and the eternal row about logic could go on.

KNURD TO NERD

The word nerd originally appeared in a Dr. Seuss story, *If I Ran The Zoo*, in 1950. After this, like all living things, it evolved. A satisfying definition connects it with the word knurd, which is 'drunk' backwards and was a campus term for those who actually studied, rather than reveled their college years away. It's not a big jump from knurd to nerd, as it is used today.

STAR TREK fans could get nerdy over anything, even whether they were called Trekkies or Trekkers. One answer to this, by the way, is that Trekkies are the ones that don't care what they're called.

The *TREK* fan came to exemplify the enthusiastic nerd, who would gleefully correct any non-Trekspert for referring to Mr. Spock as Dr. Spock – possibly the first serious nerd outrage attached to the show. *STAR TREK* also became one of the first shows to become celebrated for its tropes. The red-shirted crewman always dies, Spock always says things are fascinating and Jim always falls in love with the alien beauty.

In reality, there were so few glaring or laughable errors in *STAR TREK*, that this book has had to invent its own. So now it's time to voyage across the neutral zone of indifference and prove you are the kind of fan that keeps the eternal mission going...

STAR TREK: TOS

EPISODE LIST

To help you with this task, we are providing you with a list of all the original series episodes. While only eight stories are illustrated here (in bold), there is an item to find from every single episode somewhere in this book! Refresh your mind before you begin...

PILOT ONE

The Cage (First aired: Oct 4, 1988)

SEASON ONE

1. *The Man Trap* (Sep 8, 1966)
2. *Charlie X* (Sep 15, 1966)
3. *Where No Man Has Gone Before* (Sep 22, 1966 – pilot two)
4. *The Naked Time* (Sep 29, 1966)
5. *The Enemy Within* (Oct 6, 1966)
6. *Mudd's Women* (Oct 13, 1966)
7. *What Are Little Girls Made Of?* (Oct 20, 1966)
8. *Miri* (Oct 27, 1966)
9. *Dagger Of The Mind* (Nov 3, 1966)
10. *The Corbomite Maneuver* (Nov 10, 1966)
11. *The Menagerie Part I* (Nov 17, 1966)
12. *The Menagerie Part II* (Nov 24, 1966)
13. *The Conscience Of The King* (Dec 8, 1966)
14. *Balance Of Terror* (Dec 15, 1966)
15. *Shore Leave* (Dec 29, 1966)
16. *The Galileo Seven* (Jan 5, 1967)
17. *The Squire Of Gothos* (Jan 12, 1967)
18. *Arena* (Jan 19, 1967)
19. *Tomorrow Is Yesterday* (Jan 26, 1967)
20. *Court Martial* (Feb 2, 1967)
21. *The Return Of The Archons* (Feb 9, 1967)
22. *Space Seed* (Feb 16, 1967)
23. *A Taste Of Armageddon* (Feb 23, 1967)
24. *This Side Of Paradise* (Mar 2, 1967)
25. ***The Devil In The Dark* (Mar 9, 1967)**
26. *Errand Of Mercy* (Mar 23, 1967)
27. *The Alternative Factor* (Mar 30, 1967)
28. ***The City On The Edge Of Forever* (Apr 6, 1967)**
29. *Operation: Annihilate!* (Apr 13, 1967)

SEASON TWO

1. ***Amok Time* (Sep 15, 1967)**
2. *Who Mourns For Adonais?* (Sep 22, 1967)
3. *The Changeling* (Sep 29, 1967)
4. *Mirror, Mirror* (Oct 6, 1967)
5. *The Apple* (Oct 13, 1967)
6. *The Doomsday Machine* (Oct 20, 1967)
7. *Catspaw* (Oct 27, 1967)
8. *I, Mudd* (Nov 3, 1967)
9. *Metamorphosis* (Nov 10, 1967)
10. ***Journey To Babel* (Nov 17, 1967)**
11. *Friday's Child* (Dec 1, 1967)
12. *The Deadly Years* (Dec 8, 1967)
13. *Obsession* (Dec 15, 1967)
14. *Wolf In The Fold* (Dec 22, 1967)
15. ***The Trouble With Tribbles* (Dec 29, 1967)**
16. *The Gamesters Of Triskelion* (Jan 5, 1968)
17. ***A Piece Of The Action* (Jan 12, 1968)**
18. *The Immunity Syndrome* (Jan 19, 1968)
19. *A Private Little War* (Feb 2, 1968)
20. *Return To Tomorrow* (Feb 9, 1968)
21. *Patterns Of Force* (Feb 16, 1968)
22. *By Any Other Name* (Feb 23, 1968)
23. *The Omega Glory* (Mar 1, 1968)
24. *The Ultimate Computer* (Mar 8, 1968)
25. *Bread And Circuses* (Mar 15, 1968)
26. *Assignment: Earth* (Mar 29, 1968)

SEASON THREE

1. *Spock's Brain* (Sep 20, 1968)
2. **The Enterprise *Incident* (Sep 27, 1968)**
3. *The Paradise Syndrome* (Oct 4, 1968)
4. *And The Children Shall Lead* (Oct 11, 1968)
5. *Is There No Truth In Beauty?* (Oct 18, 1968)
6. *Spectre Of The Gun* (Oct 25, 1968)
7. ***Day Of The Dove* (Nov 1, 1968)**
8. *For The World Is Hollow And I Have Touched The Sky* (Nov 6, 1968)
9. *The Tholian Web* (Nov 15, 1968)
10. *Plato's Stepchildren* (Nov 22, 1968)
11. *Wink Of An Eye* (Nov 29, 1968)
12. *The Empath* (Dec 6, 1968)
13. *Elaan Of Troyius* (Dec 20, 1968)
14. *Whom Gods Destroy* (Jan 3, 1969)
15. *Let That Be Your Last Battlefield* (Jan 10, 1969)
16. *The Mark Of Gideon* (Jan 17, 1969)
17. *That Which Survives* (Jan 24, 1969)
18. *The Lights Of Zetar* (Jan 31, 1969)
19. *Requiem For Methuselah* (Feb 14, 1969)
20. *The Way To Eden* (Feb 21, 1969)
21. *The Cloud Minders* (Feb 28, 1969)
22. *The Savage Curtain* (Mar 7, 1969)
23. *All Our Yesterdays* (Mar 14, 1969)
24. *Turnabout Intruder* (Jun 3, 1969)

STAR TREK™

QUIBBLES WITH TRIBBLES

***IN THE 23RD CENTURY, THE STARSHIP* ENTERPRISE,** under the command of Captain James Kirk, pursues a five-year mission to explore strange new worlds. Along the way, they encounter the Klingons, an alien race with no love of the Federation – and especially no love for Kirk, who regularly obstructs their diabolical schemes.

The Klingons hatch a plan to ruin Kirk's mission by planting a deadly device – an exploding robotic tribble – at the scene of many of his most crucial assignments. Captain Kirk and his crew must hunt down the exploding tribble at each location, from planet Janus VI to Vulcan itself, to prevent cosmic catastrophe.

At the same time, to prove you are the greatest *STAR TREK* fan ever, tackle the other puzzles on every page and keep a tally of your score.

It's time to boldly go...

The Trouble With Tribbles

Faster than you can say quadrotriticale, the *Enterprise* makes it to Deep Space Station K-7. Where better to hide a deadly exploding tribble than among a whole tribulation of tribbles? **Can you help the *Enterprise* team find the furry fiend? Last one to do so is a Denebian Slime Devil!**

NERD ALERT

This is not a drill! There are FIVE SERIOUS CONTINUITY ERRORS in this picture. It could be a character in the wrong scene, a dodgy uniform, or something totally un-*TREK*-like! **Can you spot them?**

THE ARTIFACT INCIDENT

Spread across this book are 79 ARTIFACTS – one from every single episode of the original series. Their displacement in space and time threatens the very fabric of reality! **Can you find ten items here, naming the episode each one comes from?**

The Devil In The Dark

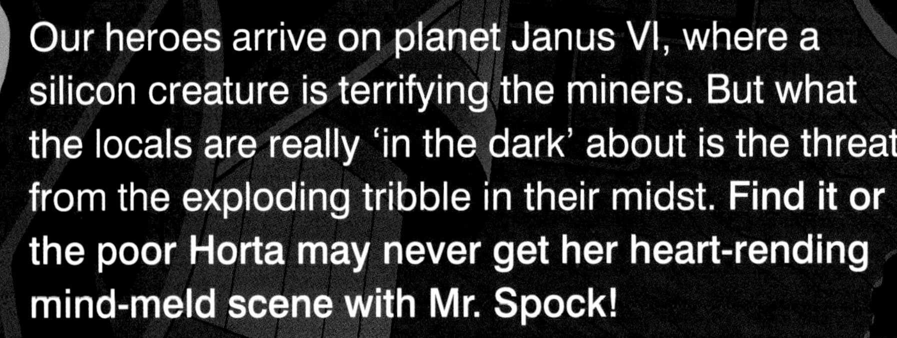

Our heroes arrive on planet Janus VI, where a silicon creature is terrifying the miners. But what the locals are really 'in the dark' about is the threat from the exploding tribble in their midst. **Find it or the poor Horta may never get her heart-rending mind-meld scene with Mr. Spock!**

THE ARTIFACT INCIDENT

Spread across this scene are TEN ARTIFACTS from other episodes of the original series. **Full sensor scan to locate them!**

NERD ALERT

Set your brains to nitpicky. There are FIVE CONTINUITY ERRORS in this scene – **spot them before they warp the fabric of space and time.**

A Piece Of The Action

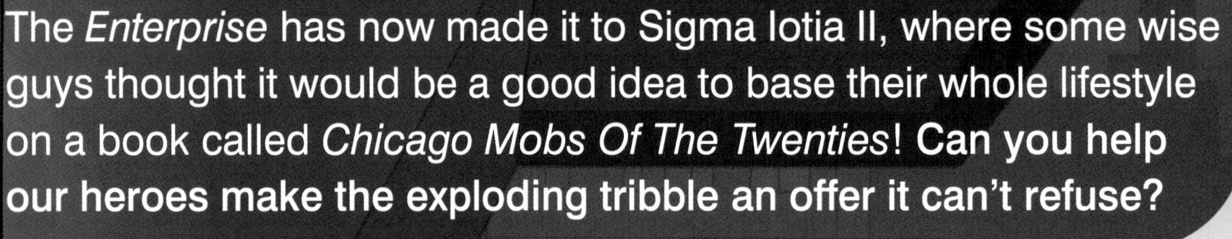

The *Enterprise* has now made it to Sigma Iotia II, where some wise guys thought it would be a good idea to base their whole lifestyle on a book called *Chicago Mobs Of The Twenties*! **Can you help our heroes make the exploding tribble an offer it can't refuse?**

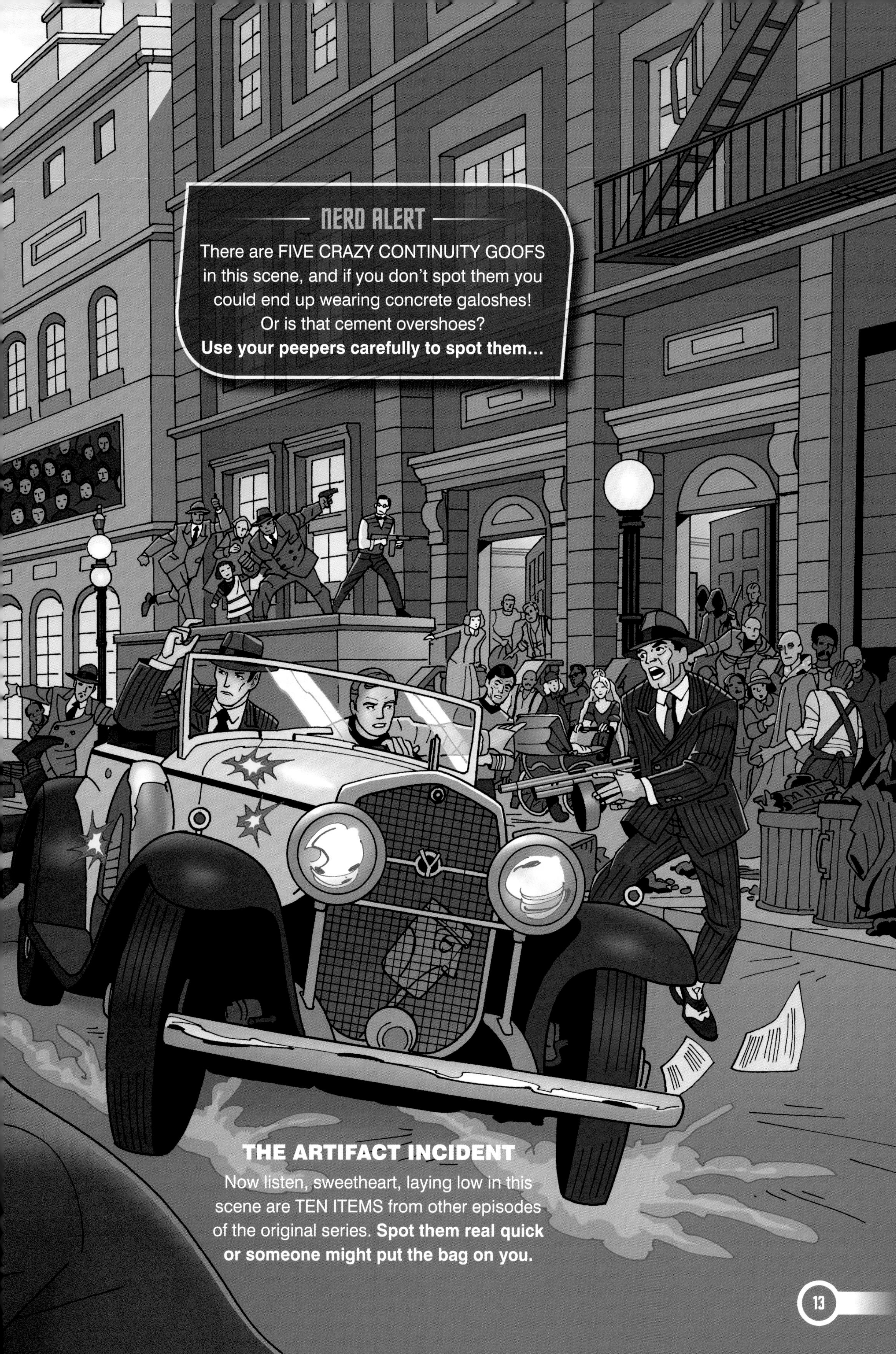
NERD ALERT
There are FIVE CRAZY CONTINUITY GOOFS in this scene, and if you don't spot them you could end up wearing concrete galoshes! Or is that cement overshoes?
Use your peepers carefully to spot them…
THE ARTIFACT INCIDENT
Now listen, sweetheart, laying low in this scene are TEN ITEMS from other episodes of the original series. **Spot them real quick or someone might put the bag on you.**

Journey To Babel

What could be trickier than a tense diplomatic reception on board the *Enterprise*? Perhaps one with Mr. Spock's father Sarek involved. **Or maybe one with an exploding tribble to find among the cosmic hors d'oeuvres!**

NERD ALERT

This is no time to be diplomatic. If you spot a CONTINUITY ERROR in this scene, point it out, fast. There are five as usual. **They could be costume errors, cast blunders or people in the wrong place at the wrong time...**

The Enterprise *Incident*

Captain Kirk has brought the *Enterprise* into Romulan space, where the crew faces almost certain destruction. Is he secretly after the Romulan cloaking device? **Or is he on the trail of the latest exploding tribble?**

NERD ALERT
The Romulans do not take kindly to people trespassing across the Neutral Zone, so spot the FIVE CONTINUITY ERRORS and get out quick. **Take too long and you might have to use the Vulcan Death Grip to escape – and that really would create a galactic incident!**
THE ARTIFACT INCIDENT
Space – the final frontier… hopefully it won't take you a five-year mission to spot the TEN OUT-OF-CONTEXT ITEMS **from other classic episodes…**

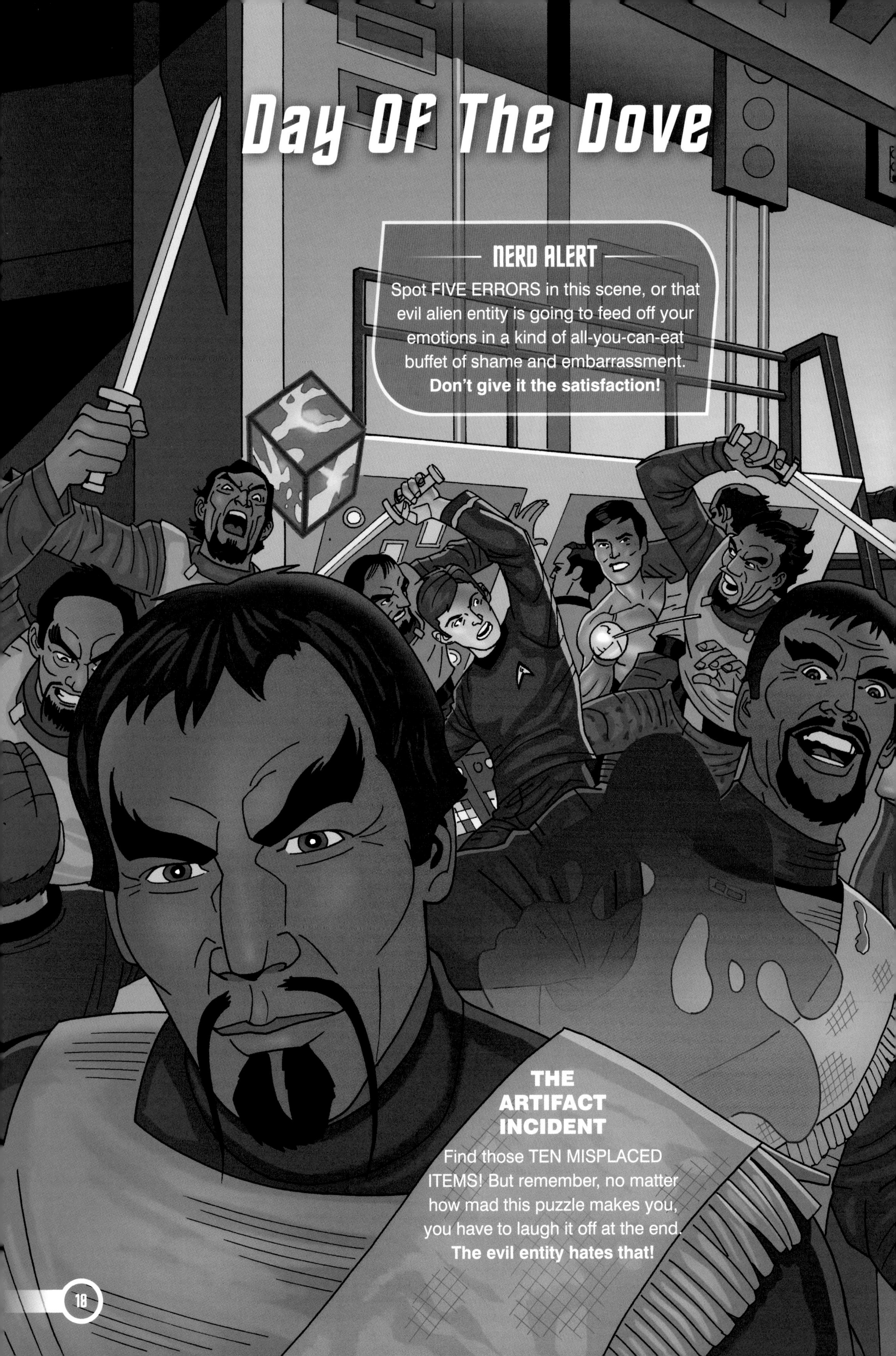
Day Of The Dove
NERD ALERT
Spot FIVE ERRORS in this scene, or that evil alien entity is going to feed off your emotions in a kind of all-you-can-eat buffet of shame and embarrassment.
Don't give it the satisfaction!
THE ARTIFACT INCIDENT
Find those TEN MISPLACED ITEMS! But remember, no matter how mad this puzzle makes you, you have to laugh it off at the end.
The evil entity hates that!

The *Enterprise* has been invaded by Klingon Commander Kang and his crew, plus an alien entity that lives on violent emotions – not an ideal combination!
The crew must fight to win back control of the Engineering Section – and spot that exploding tribble at the same time…
FIED MATERIAL
NOT OPEN

The City On The Edge Of Forever
NERD ALERT
It isn't the incredible time distortions that threaten reality as know it, but the presence of FIVE CONTINUITY ERRORS in one of the most popular episodes of all time!
They have to be spotted before the Federation itself vanishes from existence.

Ripples in time bring Kirk and his crew to the Guardian of Forever. It can take you to any time or place you wish to visit! But could it be that the captain is more worried about the exploding tribble? **Spot the furry fiend before all of history is changed!**
THE ARTIFACT INCIDENT
Finding all TEN ITEMS is a tough challenge. **Mr. Spock might agree it's easier than constructing a mnemonic memory circuit using stone knives and bearskins...**

Amok Time

Welcome to Vulcan where Mr. Spock has been called by the ancient ritual of Pon Farr. In a weird twist, his scheming betrothed, T'Pring, has made him fight a duel with Jim. **Imagine having to do that – AND find an exploding tribble!**

THE ARTIFACT INCIDENT

There are 79 stories in the original series, and eight puzzles in this book. So logic dictates you have NINE MORE ROGUE ELEMENTS to find. **Locate them and the Vulcan people will be quietly impressed with you… for a human, anyway.**

NERD ALERT
Calm your emotions and find the FIVE CONTINUITY ERRORS! The Vulcans are a peace-loving people, **but they won't accept illogical and erroneous events during their sacred rituals...**

ANSWERS

The Trouble With Tribbles [S2.15]

Greetings, nerdlings. Your quest for the impossible dream of 1701 points begins here. We begin our adventure out of chronological sequence (to annoy nerds further) with one of the most popular episodes of all time, written by David Gerrold...

TRIBBLE HUNT: C6

FIVE CONTINUITY ERRORS

1. Grid reference C4. A Klingon, in the center of the scene, is happily stroking a contented tribble. No way – they hate each other!

2. E6. Captain Kirk is wearing a uniform from *STAR TREK: DISCOVERY*. Uniforms change a lot in the 2250s and 60s. Sometimes in the original series they even change back and forth between episodes, but we haven't seen Kirk in this style of uniform yet.

3. D4. A Vulcan customer, in front of the tribble-stroking Klingon, is eating a chicken leg. Not going to happen. Vulcans are vegetarians. Spock does eat meat in 'All Our Yesterdays' (S3.23), but this is explained away as him having traveled back in time and having been telepathically influenced by his ancestors (the way you are).

4. B4. There is a giant tribble in the scene. These are not in the original series, but appear in an episode of *STAR TREK: THE ANIMATED SERIES*, 'More Tribbles, More Troubles' (*TAS* S1.5), also written by David Gerrold. There's an extra quibble about this tribble. Gene Roddenberry declared that the animated series wasn't canon, so technically it's not even part of the *STAR TREK* universe.

5. C3. Quark from *STAR TREK: DEEP SPACE NINE* is serving behind the bar. Wrong! Although other *DS9* characters visit this story in 'Trials And Tribble-ations' (*DS9* S5.6), Quark does not go back in time to the station. Just for fun, did you spot Captain Sisko, Jadzia Dax and Worf? These aren't mistakes – as time travelers, they could have been here.

TEN OUT-OF-CONTEXT ITEMS FROM OTHER EPISODES

6. F3. Tiny aliens Sylvia and Korob from 'Catspaw' (S2.7) are among the tribbles.

7. D4. These cuboctahedral blocks are from 'By Any Other Name' (S2.22).

8. E1. The cute unicorn dog (Alfa 177 canine) is from 'The Enemy Within' (S1.5).

9. C5. Near the back, a Klingon is wielding a Lirpa, (Vulcan weapon) from 'Amok Time' (S2.1).

10. C7. Almost buried is the 'Salt Vampire' from M-113, featured in 'The Man Trap' (S1.1). This also turns up in 'The Squire Of Gothos' (S1.17) where it's decorating Trelane's manor. Technically, since it could make itself look like anyone, it could be in all the other artworks, too. But, as it was the last of its kind, it should never have reappeared after 'The Man Trap' unless Professor Crater was wrong.

11. F2. These silicon eggs are from 'The Devil In The Dark' (S1.25).

12. B7. This is the boxing poster from 'The City On The Edge Of Forever' (S1.28). The Kid McCook versus Mike Mason bout, at Madison Square Garden, dates the episode to 1930.

13. C6. Let's have a salute for the Terran Empire symbol from 'Mirror, Mirror' (S2.4).

14. C1. This is the Balok dummy from 'The Corbomite Maneuver' (S1.10).

15. B7. Rear right, Adam and band are singing – from 'The Way To Eden' (S3.20). Yea, brother!

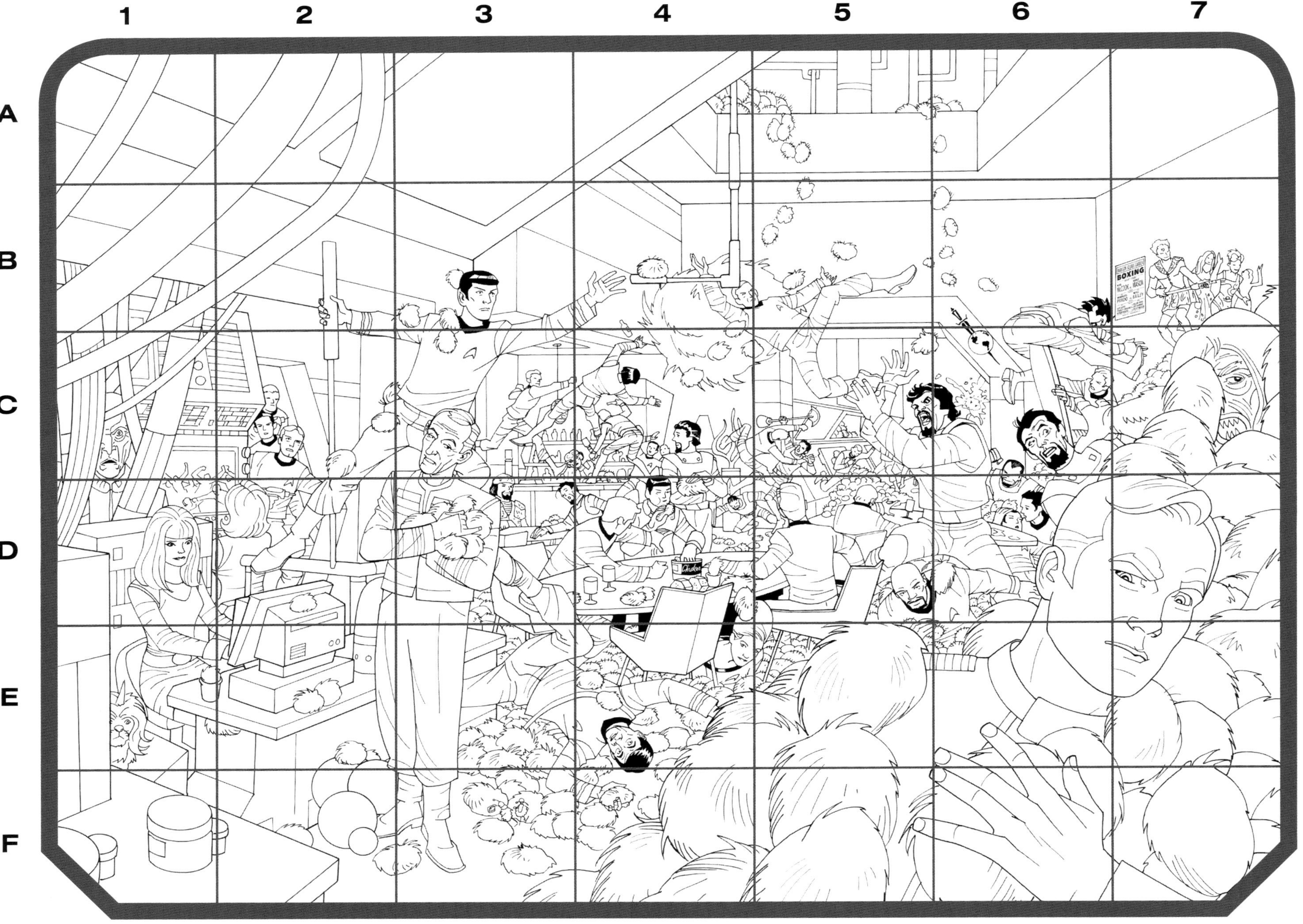
1
2
3
4
5
6
7
A
B
C
D
E
F
BOXING

The Devil In The Dark [S1.25]

This is one of the scariest episodes, yet one which still left everyone with a warm glow (especially the miners who were the Horta's early victims). Despite this being a great 'Spock' episode, it was not the first use of the Vulcan mind-meld, which actually takes place in 'Dagger Of The Mind' (S1.9).

TRIBBLE HUNT: C5

FIVE CONTINUITY ERRORS

1. E1. Chekov is in the landing party. Not likely! This story is from Season One, and Chekov does not appear until Season Two. His absence in the first series is a bit of a problem for the show, because in *STAR TREK II: THE WRATH OF KHAN*, Khan claims to recognize him, even though Chekov hadn't made his debut when Khan was on the *Enterprise*. Maybe Chekov was there, but he wasn't assigned to the bridge, so we never saw him... Anyway – he definitely isn't part of the landing party that goes to Janus VI.

2. C3. Spock is wearing a uniform from 'The Menagerie' (S1.11/12) – an earlier era. Illogical! No wonder he's frowning!

3. E5. In the cave, the Horta has written: "I NO KILL." It should say "NO KILL I."

4. F5. There should not be a sweet, little baby Horta in this scene (front right). They hatch after Spock has made friends with their mum. Incidentally, did you know that the Horta costume made its debut in a 1965 episode of *The Outer Limits*, playing a giant microbe? Also, we don't really know what baby Hortas look like since they never appear on screen.

5. E5. The Horta does not have eyes!

TEN OUT-OF-CONTEXT ITEMS FROM OTHER EPISODES

6. C5. Did you recognize the cave entrance from 'The Apple' (S2.5)?

7. D3. Jim has the phaser rifle from 'Where No Man Has Gone Before' (S1.3). Kirk definitely didn't have this, although you might wonder why not. Bizarrely, the phaser rifle only ever appears in one episode of the original series, although they used them all the time on *TNG*.

8. C3. One of several glowing phenomena in the original series, the Companion from 'Metamorphosis' (S2.9) lurks at the back.

9. E2. The spore-spraying flowers from 'This Side Of Paradise' (S1.24) are here.

10. C6. Hovering top right is Flint's robot from 'Requiem For Methuselah' (S3.19).

11. D6. Below that is the Excalbian rock creature from 'The Savage Curtain' (S3.22).

12. C2. Between Bones and Jim, we can see the symbol from 'For The World Is Hollow And I Have Touched The Sky' (S3.8). By the way, yes… this is the longest episode title, though *STAR TREK: DEEP SPACE NINE* came close to beating it with 'Looking For Par'Mach In All The Wrong Places' (*DS9* S5.3).

13. D6. Yes, you in the funny hat. It's a guard from 'The Cloud Minders' (S3.21).

14. D3. Looking at home in our cave location is Zarabeth from 'All Our Yesterdays' (S3.23).

15. B1. Oh, my paws and whiskers! Don't tell me you missed the white rabbit from 'Shore Leave' (S1.15)?

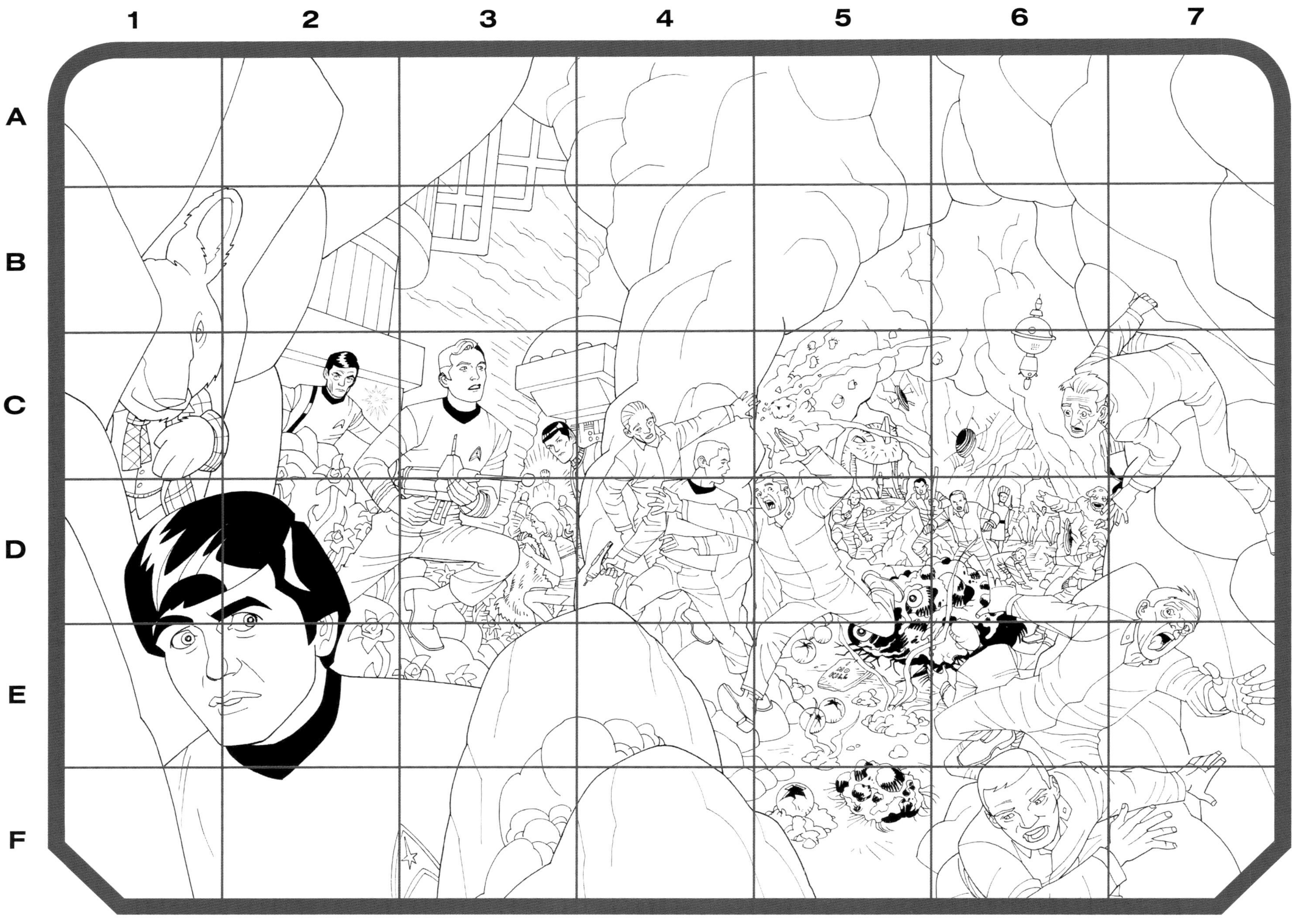
1
2
3
4
5
6
7
A
B
C
D
E
F

A Piece Of The Action (S2.17)

Let's see how wise you guys really are. Another story which regularly turns up in 'best-of' lists. This episode also created the card game Fizzbin, which has been baffling fans in their attempt to play it ever since. Remember, the second card is turned up, except on Tuesdays...

TRIBBLE HUNT: F2

FIVE CONTINUITY ERRORS

1. D5. Kirk and Spock should not be driving away in the car, during Krako's hit on Oxmyx's turf. This happens later.

2. E3. Uhura should not be there, she stays on the ship.

3. D2. The book, *Chicago Mobs of the Twenties*, is falling from the coat of the kid in the street. In fact, it was kept inside Oxmyx's office as a precious artifact. Just how detailed must that book be? It seems to have enough information for the Sigma Iotians to have accurately copied dozens of costumes, built entire streets and recreated 20th century technology including cars. By the way, writer Ron Moore pitched a sequel to this story, where the *DS9* crew visits the planet to discover that the Sigma Iotians have now based their entire society on the original series and everyone is pretending to be Kirk, Spock or McCoy.

4. C1. Picard and Data have dropped by to case the joint. But they should be in 'The Big Goodbye' (*TNG* S1.12).

5. D5. Spock should not be in his gangster suit this early in the story. Or at least Kirk should not be in Starfleet uniform when he's in the car with Spock. Take points for either!

TEN OUT-OF-CONTEXT ITEMS FROM OTHER EPISODES

6. D3. The shuttlecraft should not be in the street – it is from 'The Galileo Seven' (S1.16). As its name would not have been visible in the view we gave you of it, we added an out-sized spear stuck in the roof to be helpful, although technically this never happened in the episode.

7. C5. This might be the toughest spot in the book. The cloaking device from 'The *Enterprise* Incident' (S3.2) should not be on top of the street lamp in the middle! It's well-hidden, but hey – it is a cloaking device.

8. D7. Right of background is Ruk the android from 'What Are Little Girls Made Of?' (S1.7).

9. C5. Above Spock's hat is Alexander the Dwarf from 'Plato's Stepchildren' (S3.10).

10. D6. Pushing a pram on the sidewalk is Eleen from 'Friday's Child' (S2.11). Of course, she didn't have a pram in the actual episode, and it's unlikely they existed on her world, which had no sidewalks to push one on.

11. C7. The Lawgivers from 'Return Of The Archons' (S1.21) are in the doorway.

12. D4. A creature from 'Operation: Annihilate!' (S1.29) is on the back of a poor mug falling in the street.

13. D3. In the blue uniform, a faceless crew member from 'Charlie X' (S1.2). She has inspired a few quibbles of her own, like without a face, how did she breathe?

14. C4. In the window are the many faces from 'The Mark Of Gideon' (S3.16).

15. E6. Behind the car grille is the mask from 'The Conscience Of The King' (S1.13).

1
2
3
4
5
6
7
A
B
C
D
E
F
Chicago Mobs of the Twenties
NC-1701

Journey To Babel (S2.10)

Welcome to the Ambassadors' reception, in the episode famous for introducing Sarek, Spock's Vulcan father, and Amanda, his human mother. Mark Lenard was given the part of Spock's dad, although in reality he was just seven years older than his 'son.'

TRIBBLE HUNT: D6

FIVE CONTINUITY ERRORS

1. C4. Sarek is wearing the wrong outfit; this is his uniform on boarding the *Enterprise* earlier.

2. D5. There is a Trill at the reception, the same race as Dax from *DS9*. But this race did not appear in the original series!

3. D1. Mr. Arex from *STAR TREK: THE ANIMATED SERIES* is at the reception. He didn't join the series until it became a cartoon.

4. E3. Ambassador Gav is dead on the floor with a broken neck. This happens later. Also, his uniform coloring has been reversed. Well, in all the mayhem we didn't think it fair to expect nerds to attribute his falling over to continuity error. Score points for spotting either (not both)!

5. C7. Michael Burnham from *DISCOVERY* is at the reception just behind Amanda. She does not appear in the original series. And, as *DISCOVERY* fans will know, she would not have received an invitation as no one will ever mention her name, because of that sphere data and the time travel business.

TEN OUT-OF-CONTEXT ITEMS FROM OTHER EPISODES

6. C5. The Mugato from 'A Private Little War' (S2.19) is in the background, behind the Gorn. By the way, did you know that the Mugato was originally going to be called the Gumato, but DeForest Kelley kept saying it wrong so they changed the name?

7. C5. We hope you spotted the Gorn from 'Arena' (S1.18).

8. C6. Marla's sculpture from 'Space Seed' (S1.22) is in the background. Real nerds will have pointed out it's much too big, also.

9. D2. Reaching for the buffet is Ambassador Petri from 'Elaan Of Troyius' (S3.13).

10. D5. Miranda Jones is front right from 'Is There No Truth In Beauty?' (S3.5). Of course, Dr. Jones looks remarkably like Dr. Ann Mulhall and Dr. Pulaski, both of whom were also played by Diana Muldaur.

11. C2. Prefect Jaris from 'Wolf In The Fold' (S2.14) is not invited!

12. D2. Those brains on the table are the Providers from 'The Gamesters Of Triskelion' (S2.16).

13. C3. Causing some panic is the creature from 'Obsession' (S2.13), another of the numerous glowing, cloudy phenomena from the series!

14. E2. Did you see the telepathic sphere from 'Return To Tomorrow' (S2.20)?

15. C4. The unforgettable face of Captain Christopher Pike can be glimpsed through the crowd – he's from 'The Menagerie' (S1.11/12).

Super Quibble 1: C3. Spock should not be holding a teddy bear with fangs. Super nerds will know his mother claims in this episode that as a child he used to have a "sort of a… a fat teddy bear." Spock comments that the teddy bears on Vulcan are "alive and they have six-inch fangs." However, when we meet a real sehlat in *STAR TREK: THE ANIMATED SERIES* and *STAR TREK: ENTERPRISE* episode 'The Forge' (*ENT* S4.7), it is more like a saber-toothed tiger. Score Super Quibble points if you spotted this (and knew the reference)!

Super Quibble 2: C2. Did you notice that Prefect Jaris is acting as if possessed by Redjac? Real Treksperts will have a problem with that – he was never possessed in the episode!

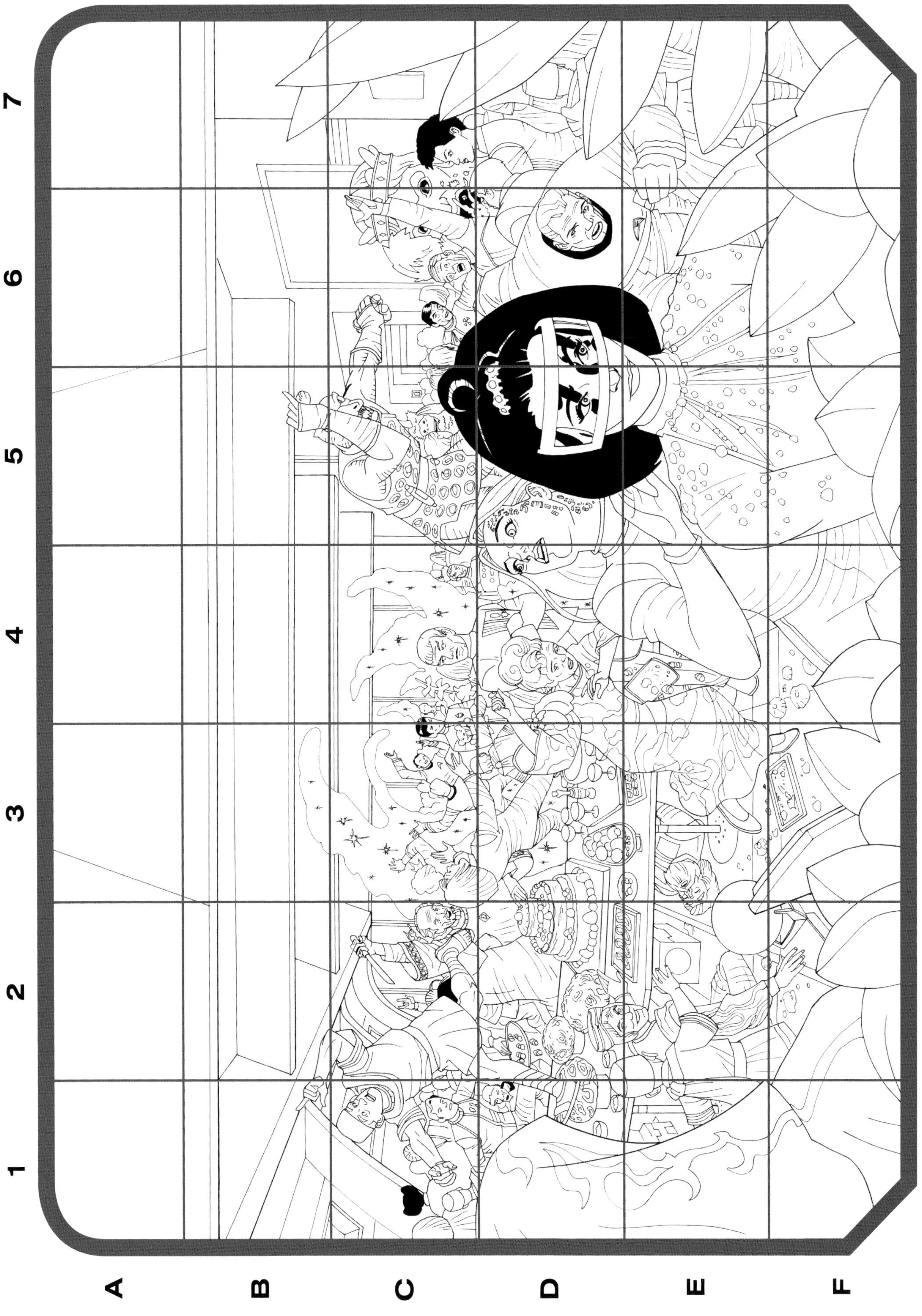

1 2 3 4 5 6 7

A B C D E F

The Enterprise Incident [S3.2]

This scene slightly misrepresents the tense character-drama of the episode, sometimes quibbled over by fans as Spock appears to be behaving out of character when he dallies with the Romulan commander. She does not even get a name in the episode, and sadly doesn't appear in our space battle.

TRIBBLE HUNT: E4

FIVE CONTINUITY ERRORS

1. D3. This *Enterprise* is the version from *STAR TREK: THE MOTION PICTURE*.

2. E3. The *Enterprise* is depicted firing a photon torpedo here – it doesn't.

3. C3. There is debris from a damaged ship – none were destroyed like this. We will also accept there was no meteorite storm at this time, instead!

4. E5. There should not be a Klingon Empire symbol on the underside of a Bird-of-Prey.

5. D6. Figures in space are wearing space suits from *STAR TREK: FIRST CONTACT*.

TEN OUT-OF-CONTEXT ITEMS FROM OTHER EPISODES

6. E6. A big hand for you if you identified the giant glowing mitt from 'Who Mourns For Adonais?' (S2.2).

7. F6. The Earth is shown from 'Assignment: Earth' (S2.26). Earth is not in Romulan space. Or, in theory, it could also be Miri's planet from 'Miri' (S1.8) or Earth from 'Tomorrow Is Yesterday' (S1.19), but this is the way the view of Earth from space was presented in S2.26.

8. C1. The planet killer from 'The Doomsday Machine' (S2.6) is passing through.

9. A1. The Tholian Web appears from 'The Tholian Web' (S3.9)! It's Tholian, and it's a web.

10. E4. On a passing space rock is the obelisk from 'The Paradise Syndrome' (S3.3). Ironically, it's an asteroid deflector, so it obviously isn't doing a very good job.

11. C6. The giant 'amoeba' from 'The Immunity Syndrome' (S2.18) takes a bow. Can an amoeba bow? Probably not.

12. E1. Did you spot the US F-104 interceptor from 'Tomorrow Is Yesterday' (S1.19)?

13. F4. Hidden among the rocks is Lazarus's one-man spacecraft from 'The Alternative Factor' (S1.27).

14. D7. This is a toughie – lurking here is Harry's spaceship from 'Mudd's Women' (S1.6).

15. D6. Floating nearby is the broken bicycle from 'Miri' (S1.8). That might be even harder!

Super Quibble 3: Did you know this episode was altered for the remastered version? In the original episode all the Romulan ships were, for production reasons, Klingon D7 battle cruisers. For the remaster, one was changed to a Romulan Bird-of-Prey. The new version is the authorized one and that's what our feature is based on. Super Quibble points for knowing the Bird-of-Prey is authentic, or for at least saying it wasn't in the original!

Adding further confusion to the 'whose spaceship?' issue is the fact that the Klingons have a Bird-of-Prey in *STAR TREK III: THE SEARCH FOR SPOCK*. They got their Bird-of-Prey as a result of an accident. In the original story for *STAR TREK III*, the villains were the Romulans. Leonard Nimoy suggested making them Klingons, but the ship stayed the same and thus the Klingons gained a Bird-of-Prey and its cloaking technology.

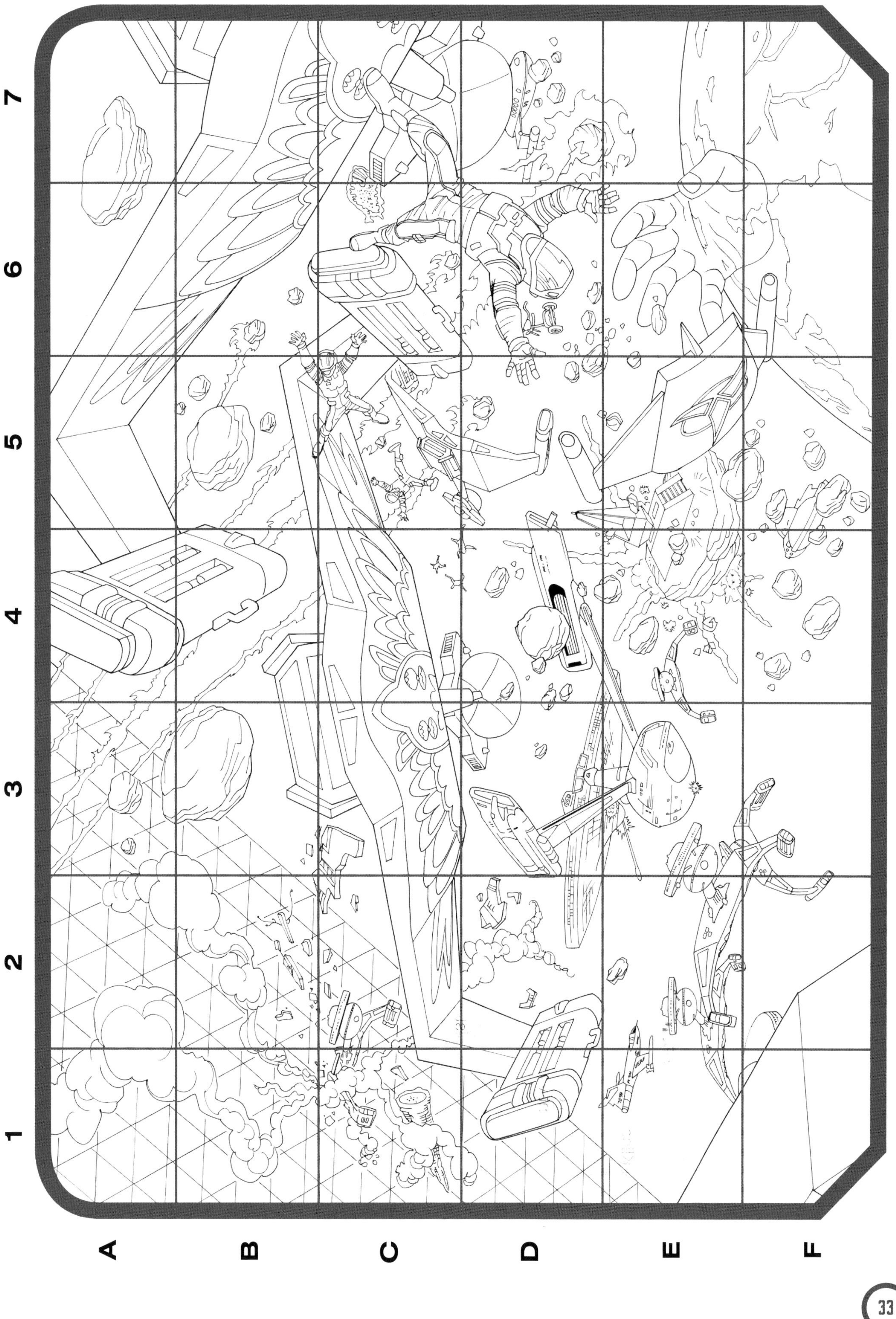

1 2 3 4 5 6 7

A B C D E F

Day Of The Dove (S3.7)

Klingon fans will be glad to see that all three Klingons who appeared in the *DS9* episode 'Blood Oath' (*DS9* S2.19) are represented in this scene… sort of. Michael Ansara appears as Kang, John Colicos (Kor) appears stage left and Billy Campbell is there as Trelane – and he played Koloth in 'The Trouble With Tribbles' (S2.15).

TRIBBLE HUNT: E6

FIVE CONTINUITY ERRORS

1. E5. The Klingon on the floor has a ridged forehead – but these did not appear in the original series! The Klingons who first hit our screens, it turns out, were affected by the Klingon augment virus that backfired and eroded the ridge feature in some. Those Klingon foreheads are still a bit of a problem. There just aren't any human-looking Klingons in the 2260s or in fact at any point in history except 2154 and 2266-2269. Best not to talk about it!

2. C5. Spock is fighting Scotty. This did happen, but it was up on the bridge. By the way, did you know you never see all of Scotty's right hand? That's because actor Jimmy Doohan lost a finger during the Normandy landings, so he always kept Scotty's right hand closed or hidden.

3. D6. A crewman is firing a phaser – but the Entity had replaced them with swords.

4. D4. Klingon Kang is laughing at the Entity. He did, but only after the battle!

5. D7. Chekov is menacing Mara – this happened, but in a corridor away from the fight scene.

TEN OUT-OF-CONTEXT ITEMS FROM OTHER EPISODES

6. D7. A drink cup with a tribble in it from 'The Trouble With Tribbles' (S2.15).

7. C3. Sulu is doing great work with that rapier but it's from 'The Naked Time' (S1.4).

8. F4. Crate Scott! That's the box van Gelder hides in, from 'Dagger Of The Mind' (S1.9).

9. D1. Kor is a great Klingon commander – but he's from 'Errand Of Mercy' (S1.26). By the way, the producers originally wanted to feature Kor in this episode but the actor who played him, John Colicos, wasn't available. He was probably filming *Anne of a Thousand Days*, which starred Geneviève Bujold, who was originally down to play Captain Janeway.

10. C4. This gladiator is from 'Bread And Circuses' (S2.25). If you knew that, celebrate with some broiled sparrow.

11. C4. Enjoying the swordplay is General Trelane – but you can call him squire – from 'The Squire Of Gothos' (S1.17).

12. C6. Right at the back, our sentry from 'A Taste Of Armageddon' (S1.23).

13. C2. Paying a visit, the computer cube from 'That Which Survives' (S3.17).

14. C6. Did you recognize Nomad from 'The Changeling' (S2.3)? If not, insufficiency existed in your response!

15. D6. Here's another upstart machine, but a tougher spot: the M5 Multitronic unit from 'The Ultimate Computer' (S2.24).

1
2
3
4
5
6
7
A
B
C
D
E
F
LFIED MATERIAL
NOT OPEN

The City On The Edge Of Forever (S1.28)

Regarded as one of the best episodes ever, this time travel tale was written by sci-fi genius Harlan Ellison. If you enjoyed the ruins here, their presence in the original scene was apparently a mistake, as the set design called for 'runes.' We're not making this stuff up.

TRIBBLE HUNT: E7

FIVE CONTINUITY ERRORS

1. C4. Sulu was not in the landing party.
2. D5. Mr. Spock is wearing a woolly hat – but he picked this up later in the episode to disguise his ears on 20th Century Earth! It is often stated that Vulcans never lie, although in this case Spock was happy to prompt Jim into explaining his ears were the result of an unfortunate accident he had as a child.
3. C2. Scotty can't change the laws of physics but he has changed his outfit. He's dressed in the clothes he wears in 'Relics' (*TNG* S6.4).
4. D3. McCoy is holding a hypo as he jumps in the portal. This is wrong – he held it in an earlier scene where he accidentally pumped himself with cordrazine.
5. D5. Jim is holding a broom, but he gets this later in the episode, doing an honest day's work in 1930. Incidentally, William Shatner has gone on record as saying this is his favorite episode, along with 'The Devil In The Dark' (S1.25).

TEN OUT-OF-CONTEXT ITEMS FROM OTHER EPISODES

6. C6. Finney from 'Court Martial' (S1.20) is front right, looking for the exploding tribble!
7. D7. Everybody loves the blue Talosian singing plant from 'The Cage' (Pilot One). Well, everybody except Philippa Georgiou, who in *DISCOVERY* episode 'If Memory Serves' (*DIS* S2.8) remarked that in the Mirror Universe she had destroyed them all while Terran Emperor.
8. C2. Salute the American flag from 'The Omega Glory' (S2.23).
9. E4. Only the nerdiest would spot the UFP standard from 'And The Children Shall Lead' (S3.4).
10. D6. Behind Uhura, the lights of Zetar appear, from um… 'The Lights Of Zetar' (S3.18). Another sparkly original series phenomenon for you to enjoy.
11. C1. Scotty is carrying a claymore sword from 'Day Of The Dove' (S3.7).
12. D3. Draw! The portal image shows Wyatt Earp from 'Spectre Of The Gun' (S3.6).
13. B1. There's a Romulan Warbird in the sky from 'Balance Of Terror' (S1.14).
14. E4. The V-12 Cadillac from 'A Piece Of The Action' (S2.17) is parked among the ruins.
15. E1. Harry Mudd's throne from 'I, Mudd' (S2.8) is in the background, left. Another one for the true Treksperts!

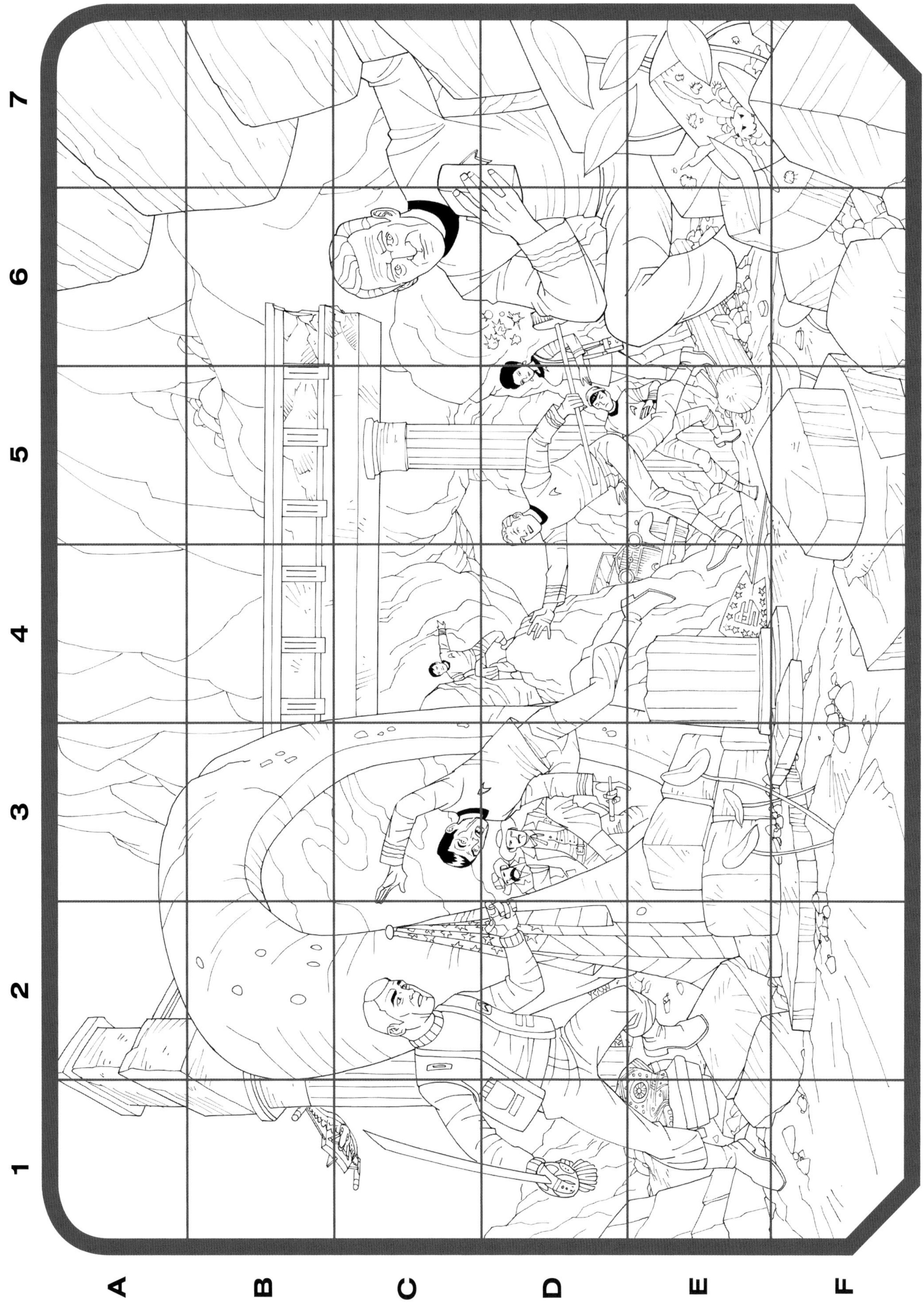

1 2 3 4 5 6 7

A B C D E F

Amok Time [S2.1]

Welcome to the planet Vulcan, for its only appearance in the original series. Spock's backstory went through some evolution and for a while his home-world was planned to be Mars. Then it was going to be called Vulcanis. Finally, Vulcan was settled on and the rest is history. Well, fictional future history…

TRIBBLE HUNT: C6

Yes, the tribble seems to have exploded in this picture. Luckily, it appears that the furry weapons seem to have achieved sentience and learned how to explode without hurting anyone. By the way, the flying debris is not a continuity error, however… just an artistic embellishment!

FIVE CONTINUITY ERRORS

1. D6. A sehlat (large, fanged bear) should not be in the scene. Depicted here is the real version of the teddy-with-fangs in the 'Journey To Babel' (S2.10) spread! This is the version of the sehlat from the animated episode 'Yesteryear' (*TAS* S1.2). It looks a lot bigger than a teddy bear, but it does have fangs.

2. C5. There should not be a Founder's Obelisk from *DS9* in the scene!

3. D3. T'Pol from *ENTERPRISE* should not be on T'Pau's throne! At one point T'Pol was going to be a young T'Pau, until the producers decided it was too complicated and T'Pol was easier to pronounce.

4. C2. A Vulcan guard has round, not pointed ears. To be honest, the Vulcans wearing helmets probably have round ears, too. The helmets were used because pointed ears were expensive to make!

5. C5. Spock is fighting with a Klingon weapon, a bat'leth, and these are from *THE NEXT GENERATION*… Also his technique is terrible. That is not how you hold a bat'leth. See the Dahar master at once.

NINE OUT-OF-CONTEXT ITEMS FROM OTHER EPISODES

6. C3. Sarek and Amanda have dropped by from 'Journey To Babel' (S2.10). It's a bit weird that they weren't here in the first place, but that's probably because they wouldn't be invented for another couple of episodes.

7. D7. The Scotty seen here is the old version from 'The Deadly Years' (S2 E12). Did ye spot that, lads and lasses?

8. C4. There's a Nazi guard from 'Patterns Of Force' (S2 E21).

9. E6. McCoy is holding the remote control for mobilizing the brainless Spock in 'Spock's Brain' (S3 E1). Just a minor quibble from the show – you can't get someone to help you with a brain transplant by wiring up their mouth first. That's not how brain surgery works, even in the 23rd century.

10. C3. Instead of T'Pring at the ceremony, we have Deela from 'Wink Of An Eye' (S3 E11). If you spotted her, it was fast work.

11. D3. A Vian from 'The Empath' (S3 E12) is fighting…

12. E3. …with the Andorian from 'Whom Gods Destroy' (S3 14).

13. D4. Bele from 'Let That Be Your Last Battlefield' (S3 E15) is refereeing the contest. But – see the Super Quibble below!

14. C7. Here's another toughie for you to finish on. Behind Scotty's head is Janice Lester's mind-swapping machine from 'Turnabout Intruder' (S3 E24)!

Super Quibble 4: The ceremonial instrument held by the figure far left, should have bells hanging from it, not balls!

Super Quibble 5: Did you notice that Bele was black down the wrong side? If you did, you are a true super nerd and we salute you.

1
2
3
4
5
6
7
A
B
C
D
E
F

HOW DID YOU DO?

Your Score

Like the Kobayashi Maru, attempting top marks in this book is something of a no-win scenario, considering the extreme difficulty of some of the puzzles. However, see where you come in our ratings:

1701 POINTS:

You are the ultimate Trekspert. You have literally saved the galaxy and are at least as clever as Mr. Spock!

301-1700:

A staggering achievement. You are a total Trekspert. Be careful the Eymorg don't try to steal your brain! Maybe you should apply for Starfleet now?

201-300:

Impressive! You may not know the rate of reproduction of a tribble, but you sure know an exploding one when you see it. You have spent your TV time well, oh nerdy one.

61-200:

Not bad! You display promise but must certainly watch the original series all over again!

0-60:

Intriguing. You attempted a *STAR TREK* puzzle book with little or no knowledge of the show at all. Your reckless optimism is admirable. Live long and prosper!

Published by Hero Collector Books, a division of Eaglemoss Ltd. 2020
1st Floor, Kensington Village, Avonmore Road W14 8TS, London, UK.

Project Concept & Management **Stella Bradley**
Designed by **Paul Montague**

For more books in the series, order online at **herocollector.com**

10 9 8 7 6 5 4 3 2 1
Printed in China.

ISBN 978-1-85875-855-8

ORANGE
CREAM
GOLD
GREEN
WHITE
YELLOW
RED CREW
RED CREW
RED
RED
PINK
CREAM
GOLD
TELEPATH SPHERE